Contents

What is alcohol?

Alcohol is a liquid. It is made of water, sugar and yeast. Drinks such as beer, spirits and wine contain alcohol.

What do we think about

Alcohol?

Jen Green

an imprint of Hodder Children's Books

Titles in the series

What do we think about ...

Adoption • Alcohol • Bullying
Death • Disability • Drugs
Family Break-Up • Our Environment

All Hodder Wayland books encourage children to read and help them improve their literacy.

- ✓ The contents page, page numbers, headings and index help locate specific pieces of information.
- ✓ The glossary reinforces alphabetic knowledge and extends vocabulary.
- ✓ The further information section suggests other books dealing with the same subject.
- ✓ Find out more about how this book is specifically relevant to the National Literacy Strategy on page 31.

Editors: Elizabeth Gogerly
Consultant: John Bennett, a Health Education Co-ordinator
Cover designer: Jan Sterling
Designer: Jean Wheeler
Photo stylist: Gina Brown
Production controller: Carol Titchener

First published in Great Britain in 1999 by Wayland (Publishers) Ltd
Reprinted in 2001 by Hodder Wayland, an imprint of Hodder Children's Books

British Library Cataloguing in Publication Data
Green, Jen
What do we think about alcohol?
1. Alcohol – Juvenile literature.
2. Alcoholism – Juvenile literature.
I. Title II. Alcohol
362.2'92

ISBN 0 7502 3421 0

Printed and bound in Hong Kong

Picture acknowledgements

Eye Ubiquitous/ John Hulme 19 (bottom); Family Life Pictures/ Angela Hampton 17; Format/ Ulrike Preuss 21, 22/ Maggie Murray 25; Martyn F. Chillmaid cover (main), title page, 11, 12, 13, 16, 19 (top), 24; Pictor International 5 (bottom) 15; Photofusion/ Paul Baldsare 20, 23; Robert Harding 9, 26; Skjold Photographs 14, 27; Tony Stone/ Steward Cohen 6/ Gerard Loucel 7/ 10, 18; Topham cover (background); Wayland Picture Library/ Tim Woodcock 4/5 (top), 8.

Many thanks to the pupils of Birchensale Middle School in Redditch, who acted as models for some of the photographs in this book

Some drinks contain more alcohol than others. Drinks such as gin and whisky have more alcohol than beer and wine.

The alcohol in all these drinks changes the way the body works, and affects how people behave.

Why drink alcohol?

Many people like to drink alcohol because it helps to make them feel happy. Some people drink to relax if they feel shy.

Other people drink alcohol because they like the taste.

Some people drink every day. Other people only drink on special occasions. This family are having some wine to celebrate a birthday.

Drinking and the body

Your body needs liquids to keep itself going. Water, milk and fruit juices help to make your body strong. Alcohol makes other kinds of changes in your body.

Alcohol can make you feel dizzy, just as you do when you spin round in circles.

Too much alcohol hurts the body. It can damage your brain, heart and liver.

How does alcohol make you feel?

Alcohol changes the way people feel. It may make them happy at first. But later, they often feel cross, upset or sad.

Drinking alcohol makes it hard to think clearly or remember things properly. The more you drink, the greater the effect.

Jo tried it and said she felt sick and sleepy.

How does alcohol make you act?

Alcohol changes the way people act too.

Walking in a straight line is easy for most of us. But alcohol makes it hard to walk in a straight line. People who have drunk too much can even find it difficult to stand up straight.

Alcohol can make it difficult to speak properly. Some people even become angry and start arguments when they drink.

Marsha's father often had fights with her mother after he'd drunk too much.

Is it safe to drink?

People who drink alcohol are more likely to do dangerous things. Simon's brother started playing about in the park after he'd been drinking. He broke his ankle.

Alcohol slows down your actions. Driving a car takes a lot of care, yet many people drive after they have had a drink.

Every year, people who have had too much to drink cause terrible accidents.

The morning after

People who have had too much to drink often feel ill the next day. This is called a hangover.

Jack's brother and sister got drunk at a party. Jack's brother had a bad headache and his sister was sick all night.

Afterwards they both felt a bit ashamed. Jack's sister said she couldn't remember anything about the party.

The drinking habit

Sometimes people drink alcohol every day to try to forget their problems. Soon they find it difficult to stop drinking and they start to drink even more alcohol.

Marsha's dad lost his job because he drank too much alcohol.

Lots of people who drink too much lose their jobs, their families and their homes.

People have drunk alcohol for thousands of years. Every country has laws that say how old you have to be before you can buy alcohol and drink in public places such as bars.

In Britain, you are allowed to drink alcohol in public if you are over 18. But your parents can give you a sip of beer or wine at home if you are over 5 years old.

Is drinking grown up?

You may have seen adverts for alcoholic drinks on TV or in magazines. They make drinking alcohol seem exciting.

Young people sometimes drink because their friends dare them to. They say that it is grown-up to drink.

But people who are drunk often act silly, not grown-up, and later feel ashamed of their stupid behaviour.

I don't drink

Many people don't drink alcohol. Daryl tried some lager but said it tasted horrible. He drinks orange or milk instead.

Some people belong to a culture or religion that does not allow drinking.

Others do not drink because they feel it will harm their health. Many athletes don't drink because they want to be fit.

Your right to choose

As you grow up, you will have to make up your own mind about drinking alcohol.

Many grown-ups like a drink every now and then. Other people don't feel they need alcohol to have fun.

At a party, friends may offer you alcohol. They may call you names if you say 'no'. But you know that alcohol can be bad for you.

You decide what you eat and drink, and you choose how you have fun.

Notes for parents and teachers

This book provides an introduction to the subject of alcohol for young children. Parents or teachers who have read the book with children may find it useful to stop and discuss issues around alcohol as they are presented by the text.

Most children are aware of alcohol from a very young age, as they see family members and other adults drinking. By the age of 10 or so, many children have had their first taste of alcohol, from sips given by parents on special occasions. Supervised drinking is seen by many parents as a way of teaching children to drink safely. Young people also learn about alcohol from information at school, from programmes and advertisements on films and TV which show people drinking. Many drinks companies try to sell their products by suggesting that it is grown-up, sophisticated, fashionable or even subversive to drink alcohol, and children are highly receptive to these ideas. Young people are naturally eager to try new experiences, particularly those associated with adulthood.

The effects of alcohol vary according to the age, sex and size of the drinker. Children, being smaller and lighter than adults, are more affected by alcohol, and the unit system by which authorities recommend 'safe' levels of drinking does not apply to them. In addition, children are inexperienced drinkers, who are not aware, for example, of the value of drinking slowly, or the dangers of mixing different kinds of drinks. Young people are more likely

than adults to drink in risky and potentially dangerous situations. Since drinking alcohol generally encourages risk-taking and recklessness, each year many children are involved in accidents after drinking alcohol.

Children learn by copying the attitudes and behaviour they see around them. It is important for parents to realize the influence that their actions have on children. Young people who see adults drinking regularly, or even getting drunk, are more likely to feel that this behaviour is acceptable. Children are also quick to notice hypocrisy, if adults' behaviour does not match the standards they expect of their children. On the other hand, setting an example of moderate drinking often helps young people to develop a sensible attitude to alcohol.

If a child in your care gets drunk or drinks against your wishes, try not to over-react to the situation. It is better to talk the incident over quietly, and find out why it happened, as well as raising the dangers of alcohol. If a family member has a drinking problem, children may feel called upon to make excuses or cover up for the person concerned. They are likely to be confused or upset if an adult becomes incoherent, or behaves erratically. The whole family will suffer if a family member becomes aggressive or argumentative after drinking. There are many organizations that offer help and support for people with a drinking problem, and their families. Some of these are listed overleaf.

Glossary

Alcohol A liquid containing yeast and sugar, which is used to make alcoholic drinks. Beer, cider, wine and spirits are all alcoholic drinks.

Hangover A word used to describe the way people sometimes feel after drinking alcohol. A person with a hangover may feel sick or have a headache, and is often very thirsty.

Liver A part of the body that helps to break down and digest food.

Spirits Types of drinks that contain high levels of alcohol. Gin, whisky, brandy and rum are all different kinds of spirits.

Further information

Books to read

Drinking Alcohol by Pete Sanders and Steve Myers (Watts/Gloucester Press, 1996)

We're Talking About Alcohol by Jenny Bryan (Wayland Publishers, 1995)

Why Do People Drink Alcohol? by Pete Sanders (Watts/Gloucester Press, 1995)

Organizations which offer help to people with drinking problems and their families:

Alcohol Concern
Waterbridge House
32-36 Loman Street
London SE1 0EE
Tel: 0171 928 7377

Al-Anon Family Groups
61 Great Dover Street
London SE1 4YF
Tel: 0171 403 0888

Use this book for teaching literacy

This book can help you in the literacy hour in the following ways:

- ✓ Children can discuss the themes and link them to their own experiences of alcohol.
- ✓ They can discuss the case studies and speculate about how they might behave in each situation.
- ✓ They can compare this book with fictional stories about alcohol to show how similar information can be presented in different ways.
- ✓ They can try rewriting some of the situations described in the form of a story.

Index

Numbers in **bold** refer to pictures as well as text.

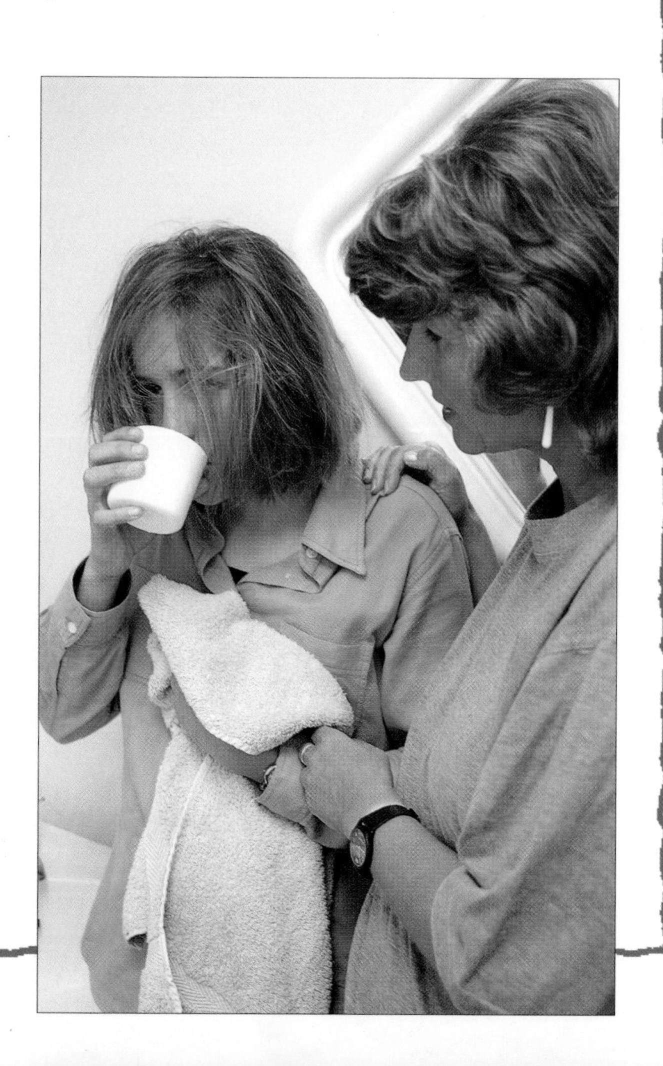